Inside
Rabbit Burrows

Liz Chung

PowerKiDS
press™

New York

Published in 2016 by The Rosen Publishing Group, Inc.
29 East 21st Street, New York, NY 10010

First Edition

Editor: Sarah Machajewski
Book Design: Mickey Harmon

Photo Credits: Cover, pp. 1 (rabbits) Paul Maguire/Shutterstock.com; cover, pp. 3–4, 6, 8, 10, 12, 14, 16, 18, 20, 22–24 (grass) Juan J. Jimenez/Shutterstock.com; cover, pp. 1, 3–4, 6–10, 12, 14, 16, 18, 20, 22–24 (magnifying glass shape) musicman/Shutterstock.com; p. 5 Patryk Kosmider/Shutterstock.com; p. 7 (rabbit) Leena Robinson/Shutterstock.com; p. 7 (inset) Matthijs Wetterauw/Shutterstock.com; p. 9 (main) Calm Listener/Shutterstock.com; p. 9 (inset white rabbit) Stefan Petru Andronache/Shutterstock.com; p. 9 (inset desert) KKimages/Shutterstock.com; p. 11 Tom Reichner/Shutterstock.com; p. 13 Cyril Ruoso/Minden Pictures/Getty Images; p. 15 Steve Shott/Dorling Kindersley/Getty Images; p. 17 (inset) Emily Veinglory/Shutterstock.com; p. 17 (main) Robert Orcutt/Shutterstock.com; p. 19 © iStockphoto.com/Diane Labombarbe; p. 21 Les Stocker/Oxford Scientific/Getty Images; p. 22 Miroslav Hlavko/Shutterstock.com.

Library of Congress Cataloging-in-Publication Data

Chung, Liz, author.
Inside rabbit burrows / Liz Chung.
     pages cm. — (Inside animal homes)
Includes bibliographical references and index.
ISBN 978-1-4994-0876-8 (pbk.)
ISBN 978-1-4994-0891-1 (6 pack)
ISBN 978-1-4994-0927-7 (library binding)
1. Rabbits—Habitations—Juvenile literature. 2. Animal burrowing—Juvenile literature. 3. Animal behavior—Juvenile literature. I. Title. II. Series: Inside animal homes.
QL737.L32C58 2016
599.32—dc23
                              2015013854

Manufactured in the United States of America

CPSIA Compliance Information: Batch #WS15PK: For Further Information contact Rosen Publishing, New York, New York at 1-800-237-9932

Contents

Under the Ground

What would it be like if your home was under the ground? This idea may seem strange for people, but it's not strange for rabbits. They dig into the ground and create a home that's big enough to house big rabbit families.

Rabbit homes are called burrows. We may only be able to see the entrance, but the inside of a rabbit's home can tell us how this creature lives. Let's check it out!

Where will this rabbit hole lead us?

Rabbits vs. Hares

Rabbits are **mammals**. There are 28 species, or kinds, of rabbits. They're part of an animal family that includes hares. Rabbits and hares are a lot alike, so people often mistake them for each other. However, they're totally different animals.

Rabbits live all over the world. They're found in North America, South America, and Europe. They also live in parts of Africa, India, and Asia. Many rabbit species originally came from Europe. They were taken to other parts of the world long ago.

THE INSIDE SCOOP

Rabbits have shorter ears, back legs, and tails than hares. Hares don't burrow like rabbits—they live above ground.

rabbit

hare

Rabbits and hares look much alike and live in the same places. It's easy to get them mixed up.

Where Do Rabbits Live?

Rabbits live in many kinds of **environments**. Some live in deserts, or hot, dry places. Other species live in tropical forests, which are very hot and wet. Rabbits live in cold, snowy environments, as well as wetlands. The environment affects how rabbit burrows look. Desert burrows are dug in sand, while forest burrows are in the dirt.

The eastern cottontail rabbit lives near people. These rabbits make their home in forests, meadows, fields, or wooded areas. However, cottontails don't burrow. They can often be seen running through our backyards looking for food!

Rabbits' bodies **adapt** to their environment. For example, a desert rabbit has a thin fur coat, while a rabbit in a cold environment might have a thicker coat.

Rabbit Body

A rabbit's most familiar feature is its long ears. They're good for hearing predators. If a rabbit hears a predator, it uses its powerful legs to run away. Its back legs are longer than its front legs. Another noticeable feature is the rabbit's fur coat. It's usually brown, but sometimes it's reddish brown or tan.

A rabbit's nose is very powerful. It's always **twitching** and picking up scents. Its eyes are on the sides of its head. They can see in all directions, including in front of and behind the rabbit.

THE INSIDE SCOOP

The pygmy rabbit is the smallest rabbit. It's 7.9 inches (20 cm) long and weighs 0.9 pound (0.4 kg). The biggest rabbits can be over 19.7 inches (50 cm) long and weigh about 4.4 pounds (2 kg).

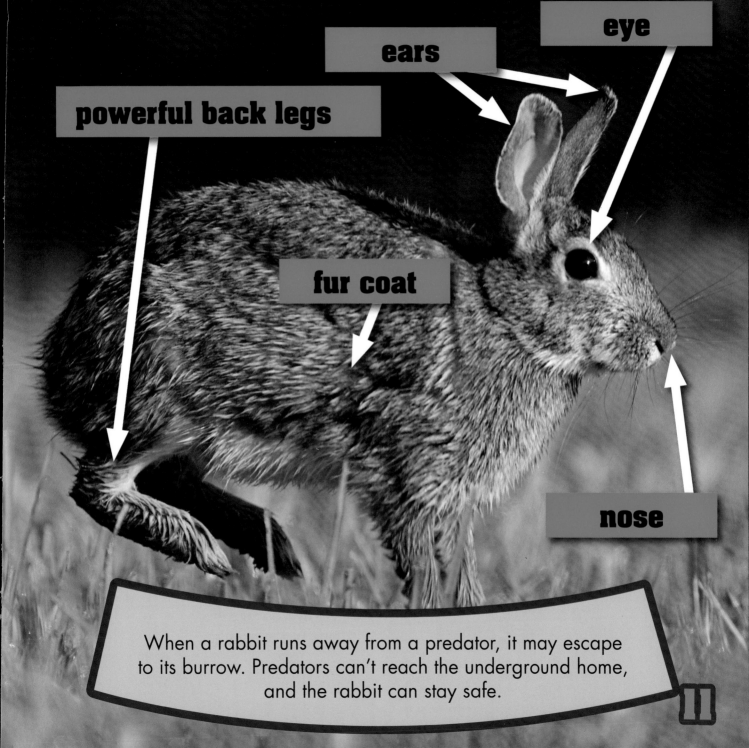

powerful back legs

ears

eye

fur coat

nose

When a rabbit runs away from a predator, it may escape
to its burrow. Predators can't reach the underground home,
and the rabbit can stay safe.

Digging It

Digging is natural for rabbits. Some species of rabbits dig burrows in the ground. Rabbits create burrows anywhere they're able to dig, such as in dirt, sand, and more.

Rabbits enter and exit a burrow through a hole in the ground. The hole leads to a tunnel. Rabbits make the tunnel long and narrow, which means predators can't follow them into their home. The tunnel leads to a big room called a chamber. This is where rabbits spend most of their time.

THE INSIDE SCOOP

Not all rabbits burrow. Nonburrowing rabbits dig surface nests called forms in the ground.

Burrows are built in areas that have a lot of food and enough cover from plants, such as grass and leaves, to hide the entrance.

All in the Family

Some rabbit species build warrens. A warren is a **network** of connected burrows. Warrens are big enough to hold large rabbit families, which are called colonies. Most rabbits are fine living alone, but some species are more social.

One rabbit species that forms colonies is the European wild rabbit. Its colony has adult male rabbits, which are called bucks. Adult female rabbits are called does. They have baby rabbits, which are called kits. At any time, a burrow likely contains all these members.

THE INSIDE SCOOP

Warrens can be as deep as 9.8 feet (3 m) under the ground.

A warren's chambers are used for nesting and sleeping.

entrance

chambers

Inside the Burrow

Rabbits spend all day in their burrow. That's because they're nocturnal. That means they sleep during the day and are active at night. Rabbits sleep in one of the burrow's chambers until it's time to wake up and find food.

Rabbits eat grass, flowers, clover, and any kind of leafy plant in the summer months. They will eat vegetables from gardens if they can get to them. In the winter when fewer plants grow, rabbits eat twigs, tree bark, and any plant they can find.

THE INSIDE SCOOP

During the day, rabbits that don't burrow sleep under low-hanging branches or brush.

Rabbits poop in their burrows, then eat it! Their poop contains **nutrients** their body didn't break down the first time.

Bunny Behavior

Rabbits have many behaviors that keep them and their colony safe. A rabbit's big ears and powerful nose help it sense danger. Rabbits communicate with, or talk to, other rabbits by thumping their leg on the ground. This warns others that danger is near.

If rabbits sense a predator, they freeze so predators can't see their movements. They also hide, staying very still until danger has passed. If a predator goes after them, rabbits run very fast and change direction often to **confuse** the predator.

THE INSIDE SCOOP

Rabbits sleep in their burrow during the day. Burrows keep rabbits hidden from animals that would otherwise eat them.

Rabbits spend all night looking for food. However, many of their predators also look for food at night. The rabbits could become their food if they're not careful.

19

Staying Safe

A rabbit's home has a very important job: **protecting** the colony. If rabbits didn't have anywhere to stay safe, their species would die out. Rabbits are food for many predators. Their population could lower quickly, but rabbits **mate** often to keep this from happening.

Rabbits mate about three to four times a year. They have between three and eight kits each time. Kits stay in the burrow for about three weeks. Their mom feeds them once a day until they can leave the burrow.

Baby rabbits are born blind, without any hair, and helpless. The burrow protects them until they can be on their own.

Rabbits in the Wild

Rabbits are popular pets, but pet rabbits are not the same as rabbits you find in the wild. They act differently, eat different foods, and their homes are different, too. Never think that you can catch a rabbit and bring it home! That would only hurt it.

The next time you see a rabbit in the wild, leave it be. It's probably out looking for food. It will return to its home in a matter of hours, where it will help its colony **survive**.

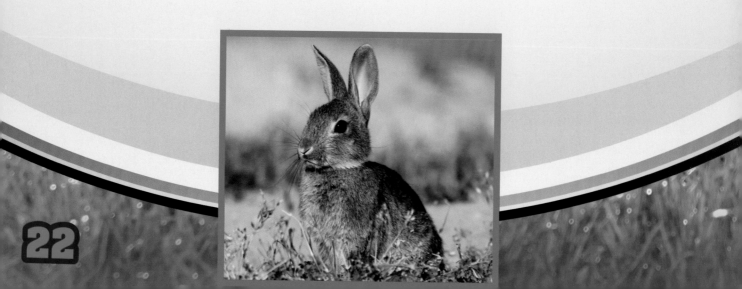

Glossary

adapt: To change to be able to better survive in an environment.

brush: Low, thick plant growth.

confuse: To cause someone to not understand or follow something.

environment: Everything in the world that surrounds a living thing.

mammal: A warm-blooded animal that has a backbone and hair, breathes air, and feeds milk to its young.

mate: To come together to make babies.

network: A system in which all the parts are connected.

nutrient: Matter important in small quantities for the nutrition of animals.

protect: To keep safe.

survive: To continue to live.

twitch: To give a short, sudden jerking movement.

Index

Websites

Due to the changing nature of Internet links, PowerKids Press has developed an online list of websites related to the subject of this book. This site is updated regularly. Please use this link to access the list: www.powerkidslinks.com/home/rabb